IRISH SUPERSTITIONS

IRISH SUPERSTITIONS

Dáithí Ó hÓgáin

Gill & Macmillan

Gill & Macmillan Ltd
Hume Avenue, Park West
Dublin 12
with associated companies throughout the world
www.gillmacmillan.ie

© *Dáithí Ó hÓgáin 1995, 2002*
978 07171 3371 0
Illustrations by Fiona Fewer
Print origination by Carole Lynch
Printed in Malaysia

This book is typeset in 10/15 pt Adobe Garamond.

The paper used in this book comes from the wood pulp
of managed forests. For every tree felled, at least one
tree is planted, thereby renewing natural resources.

*A catalogue record for this book is available
from the British Library.*

3 5 7 6 4

CONTENTS

FOREWORD — THE MIND ENGAGED

Many folk beliefs are referred to as 'superstitions', with the implication that these are silly ideas in no way connected with common sense or rational thought. However, these beliefs are related to human feeling and to psychological needs, and so — no matter how far-fetched they appear — always have something to tell about our attitudes towards life and towards the world around us.

A survey of folk beliefs makes it clear that they bear witness to two basic human emotions: fancy and fear. They are dramatic by nature, for imagination and insecurity are never-failing sources of drama. They are poetic too, focusing on images to the neglect of conscious analysis, and being carried along by whatever is felt to be cohesive in these images.

It can indeed be claimed that superstitions are nothing more than impressions strongly implanted in the mind due to a kind of speculation which mixes the surreal with the real and confuses the abstract with the concrete. They are preserved, and their hold on the mind strengthened, by assertion in speech and by repetition in practice. Though we need not take them literally, they are always of

interest, for man 'hopes and fears all', and the
unpredictability of life is just as enduring, as ever-
present, as is our fascination with it.

ONE

MAN THE SUMMATION OF ALL THINGS

*T*he sense of self is the most constant one in our experience, and much lore therefore centres on it. The human imagination has long been concerned with aspects of our lives, of our own minds and bodies. Although most of the related superstitions are not validated by modern medical science, they often gave people confidence — illusory, but none the less reassuring — in dealing with matters of immediate personal importance.

The head is master to the body

The head and face, as the most obvious and visible conveyors of personality, were given particular emphasis in body-lore. Many cultures visualised the head as the seat of the intellect but also as the seat of the emotions, because of the expression of human feeling in the face — its paling and reddening, its laughter and tears, its variety of grimaces and contortions.

The fact that the head contains the brain and therefore man's rationalising powers was clear from behaviour and from the results of injury, and perhaps was also known from vivisection. The brain is in Irish called *inchinn*, in the sense of understanding, but a double of it is *meanma*, which has connotations of temperament, and both rationale and feeling are contained in the word *intinn*, for the general mental functioning. Not surprisingly, with this notion of totality, a popular proverb stated that 'The head is master to the body,' meaning that if anything goes wrong with the head, the body will be bound to suffer in some way.

Decision — the head stands alone

In early Irish culture, the head was considered to represent the whole of the person. This attitude is shown in ancient rituals of the Celts, who, even after decapitating a foe in battle, would preserve the head and accord it special respect. Classical writers tell of the continental Celts that they were accustomed to hang the heads of their enemies from the ridge-poles of their tents, and that they brought them along to feasts as if these dead enemies were guests. Early Irish stories tell of heads speaking after death, especially at feasts, where they gave instructions and messages to their listeners.

The head seems to have had particular significance in early Ireland in the context of druids and poets, to whom knowledge of past, present and future was attributed. The famous stone head found at Corleck in Co. Cavan, dating from the

Celtic Iron Age, may reflect this: it has three faces, as if to indicate that the seer could simultaneously look into these three dimensions of time.

Information comes through the ears, is distilled in the brain, is reproduced through the mouth

Early literary sources show that the brain was regarded as the control-centre of the body. This eminently sensible view persisted down through the centuries in folklore. At all stages, of course, there was fanciful elaboration, and various attempts were made to bring the other parts of the head into the scheme of things. For example, the breath was envisaged as a stream which carries the words forward. Since it comes from deep inside the body and returns there, it could be thought of as a kind of liquid of the soul.

To breathe ritually upon an object was to impart something of one's essence to that object. This was an important element in folk healing — for example, it was widely believed in Ireland that thrush of the throat could be cured by a fasting person breathing into the patient's mouth.

The ear is prophetic

Folk tradition held that not just words but other effects could be picked up by one's ear. Thus, if the right ear were warm, it was said that the person was being praised, while heat in the left ear meant that backbiting was taking place. Such notions, described by Pliny as current in ancient Rome, remain popular in modern folklore. A belief common in all parts of Ireland was that if a tiny ringing were heard in the ear, the death of a friend was imminent. An alternative explanation was that a friend in Purgatory in need of a prayer was sending the little bell as a signal.

The power of the tongue

Words, and the proper crafting of them, have always been considered extremely important in Ireland, where there is deep respect for *dea-chaint* (good speech).

The fancy was that the tongue was the cutter and shaper of words as they passed through the mouth, and people with a long and agile tongue were thought to be very good talkers. Medieval Irish literature claims that poets had two capsules on their tongues — one full of honey for praising, the other full of poison for satirising. By a similar process of thinking, later folklore represents poets as washing their mouths after composing a particularly bitter satire. Children, of course, were often told that a spot on the tongue resulted from telling lies, and were made to wash out their mouths when they used vulgar words.

Words can either harm or help

Speech, with its immense social potential, was highly valued and also greatly feared. There was a very strong belief in the power of a 'bad tongue' — that is, the tongue of a malicious and unscrupulous person. 'Envy would eat away the hills,' went an old saying.

Defamation was also credited with more concrete effects. It was thought that venomous criticism could actually bring sickness or even death to the victim. False or sarcastic praise was feared because of its cynical intent and, accordingly, its sinister nature. Most dreaded of all were compliments which were 'craving', or laced with envy. Many stories were told of children being falsely praised by a covetous neighbour, and as a result falling very ill or dying.

The tongue could be used in constructive ways also. Those with a 'silver tongue', for instance, could give great entertainment and encouragement to their fellows, or could avail themselves or others in matters of romance by composing fine songs or rhetorics of love. The positive side too was expressed in concrete terms, such as in the belief that a lick of the tongue could heal cuts and burns, particularly if the tongue had first licked the back of a lizard — an instance of how exotic actions or materials were much valued by the popular imagination. The connection with the lizard probably results from the widespread notion that this creature is itself tongueless, and so its wasted tongue 'energy' would be gained by the person who applied his own tongue to it.

The soul can be observed

The image of the head as the centre of the life-force, and of the personality, gave rise to many other ideas. For instance, stories were told of how the soul could sometimes be seen, in the shape of a little bird, a butterfly or a bee, flying out from the mouth of a sleeping person and returning before he awoke. The person might then describe a dream which he had, a dream based on what the soul saw when it had temporarily left the body. A prevalent belief was that, at death, the soul departed through *log an bhaithis*: that is, 'the hollow in the crown of the head'.

Wisdom, like truth, will out

The general belief was that wisdom was an innate quality — a sort of shining light of the intellect — with which a small number of people were born and which marked them out from the beginning. Many Irish stories tell of a young genius speaking words of poetry or prophecy soon after his birth, to the astonishment of the adults present.

It was said that there were three qualities which came by nature and could not be properly acquired through learning: *guth, féile agus filíocht* (a singing voice, generosity and poetry).

The head examined and healed

All heads, whether of geniuses or of ordinary people, are of course susceptible to illness, which was imagined to be caused by a spirit entering the person and putting his dimensions out of proportion. It was thought that the head should have the same circumference when measured vertically and horizontally, and so in order to cure headaches or nervous tension, it was measured both ways to discover what abnormality had occurred. A bandage or stocking would then be tightened around the head and gently squeezed to bring it back into shape.

A common fancy was that the shape of the head indicated personal characteristics. For instance, a broad brow was taken to mean a very developed intelligence, whereas wrinkles on the forehead meant that a person was prone to worry and anxiety. The head was accorded importance in aesthetic terms too. In both early and modern times, a person with a broad temple, bright forehead and gradually narrowing cheeks was considered very handsome.

The mantic importance of the head was reflected in the widespread belief that cures could be obtained by drinking milk from a skull, and the custom in some areas of swearing oaths on skulls.

Blondes held in high regard

An ancient tendency among the Celtic peoples was to consider fair hair as especially beautiful, deriving from the notion that brightness was a divine trait. Both druids and heroes used lime in order to brighten their hair-colour. The seer-hero Fionn Mac Cumhaill was described as fair-haired — his very name (*fionn*) signifies this; in his case, his hair reflected the shining light of his intellect. Other-world women — who inspired the prophets and poets — were always said to have had hair of that colour.

The magic of red hair

Accounts of the early Celts show that red hair was prevalent among them, and this too was held in high regard, even though it could be considered to involve a degree of magical danger. Red, after all, is the colour of fire, one of the most inexplicable sources of support to ancient man, but also one of the most hazardous elements known to him. It is curious that, in later times, red hair was often regarded as an inheritance from the Viking raiders who settled in medieval Ireland.

In a country like Ireland, with varieties of green as the general background, the colour red is rare and therefore stands out clearly to the eye. Similarly, in any given group of people, one with red hair would be noticed. Superstitions tend to centre on the unusual, and particularly the picturesque. Thus, to meet a red-haired woman was often considered a bad portent. The belief was very strong among fishermen, who would turn back home if they met with such a woman when going to sea. Perhaps it was felt that a conspicuous woman might deflect the attention of seafarers from their dangerous tasks!

Hair indicates the person and the destiny

Red hair was also taken as an indication of a hot-blooded temperament. Since hair was thought to spring internally from the blood, for it to retain this colour was a reflection of that essential human element in its most productive and heated humour. People tended, and to an extent still tend, to regard hidden traits as being expressed externally in one's physical appearance. Strong and healthy hair, whether on the head or on the body, suggested a high degree of strength and health within the whole person.

Conversely, a decline in one's hair presaged a general decline in well-being. Balding, while it had to be accepted as inevitable, was considered extremely undesirable. An Irish saying has it that 'Baldness is most uncomely, and only blindness is a greater affliction.' A sudden greying or thinning of body hair was wont to cause alarm, as it was taken as a portent of sickness or even death.

Strength and power of the person lies in the hair

In Ireland, and in several other countries, it was thought highly unlucky for a man to allow a woman to cut his hair or shave his beard, the danger being that he would thereby lose his strength or even his virility. This belief may stem from the biblical account of Samson and Delilah, but the Samson story itself is indebted to ancient folklore of the Middle East.

Many cultures evince a secret fear of an occult power residing in women. The ultimate source of this — no doubt male — notion is difficult to decipher, but some psychoanalysts would attribute it to the symbolism of the male 'dying' in sexual intercourse. It is significant also that many primitive cultures considered women to be especially dangerous when menstruating; the association with lunar periods increased the feeling that women derived extra power from their involvement with outside agencies. Incidentally, it was thought inadvisable in Ireland and elsewhere to cut hair while the moon was waning, as this would bring about a corresponding decline in the hair.

The ancient Celts wore their hair long in battle, in the belief that their full power was thereby utilised. Down through the centuries, military leaders in many countries have made the trimming of hair and beard obligatory for their soldiers, principally for hygienic

reasons, but perhaps originally in order to deprive the enemy of the chance of seizing a soldier's hair in close combat. The Celtic custom of wearing hair long survived in Ireland for a considerable time, and men took particular pride in leaving the moustache untrimmed. Various ordinances during the reign of Elizabeth I sought to compel Irishmen to cut their moustaches, but to little avail.

Hair shows feelings, status and fate

Long hair on women was understood to express freedom and informality, and it was habitually tied up only after marriage. The hair thus symbolised a woman's sexuality. A long tradition, indeed, associated hair with sexual attraction — a lock was often given as a love-token, and strands of hair were an important ingredient in love-potions. In a different context, women allowed their hair to hang unkempt when keening the dead. On formal occasions, such as going to church, no woman would allow her hair to straggle; it would be gathered up neatly as a mark of solemnity and respect.

Since of its nature the hair can take on many shapes, its condition was much noted in folk divination. For instance, the 'cow's lick', or tuft of hair standing up over the forehead, was taken as a sign of health and intelligence in a child. On the other hand, a pronounced forelock in a woman, with the hair thinning about it, was called the 'widow's peak', and betokened the death of the woman's spouse in the near future.

Hair an intrinsic part of the body

People were very careful not to throw their severed locks into the fire, for they would feel themselves weaken as the hair burned. It was held that those who allowed their hair to burn would on the Last Day be burning their fingers in an attempt to retrieve it from the fire. This, needless to say, was derived from the Christian doctrine of the resurrection of the body. It was maintained that the best place in which to put discarded hair was a hole in the ground or a hole in the wall, from which it could be collected before the Final Judgment.

This, however, entailed its own difficulty, for if the birds were to discover it and use it in the building of their nests, severe headaches could result for the owner of the hair. Such pain had its own remedy in popular belief, and a cure for both headaches and head-colds was to discover the *ribe tuathail*, a particular strand at the back of the head, and pull it.

The eyes are a window on the mind

A well-known saying in Irish lists the three most vulnerable parts of the body as 'the eye, the knee and the elbow'. The eyes have long been considered 'the mirror of the soul', and folk fancy ranged all the way from the serious observation that one should be careful with a person whose eyes expressed a humour at variance with that of his mouth, to the more flippant one that the eye of a girl at a dance was as sharp as that of a hawk surveying a plain or of a hound after a hare! A blue-green eye-colour was regarded as very attractive, while a grey eye was an indication of prudence and practicality.

Unusual types of eyes attract suspicion

Unusual formations of the eyes were mistrusted — especially where the eyes were very close together or differed from each other in colour. To nervous and over-imaginative observers, such facial aspects suggested some hidden destructive tendency.

Belief in the 'evil eye' was prevalent since antiquity in many countries. According to this, a glance by some individuals could bring harm to whatever it was cast upon. In Ireland, it was described as a 'blinking' or a 'cutting' eye. While the supposed possessor of such an eye was sometimes considered a malicious or covetous person, it was also thought that one could possess this destructive trait due to no fault of one's own or without even knowing of it.

Once it became known to an honest person that he possessed the undesirable trait, he might strive to avoid doing damage with it. Since it was believed that the object which first met the eye in the morning would suffer the full effect of it for that day, he could carefully direct his first glance at weeds or undergrowth — which would, of course, wither away as a result of the repeated exposure.

Folk tradition tends to concentrate on the dramatic, and most stories of the evil eye told of people who used the attribute maliciously and were therefore to be avoided at all costs. It was claimed that those who acted treacherously towards their neighbours did not close their eyes, even when sleeping. A child, horse or cow which was 'overlooked' by such a person would pine away and die, and so it was advisable to procure some defence against the eye, or some remedy which would neutralise its effect. Defences and remedies included religious amulets, the Sign of the Cross, the invocation of God's blessing, and the more quaint and antique one of spitting.

The blessed power of saliva

The use of spittle as a prophylactic was widespread in human culture, and was very popular in Ireland. Since it, like the breath, comes from the mouth, it was thought to contain the essence of one's personality, and therefore of one's potential. Just as people spat on a wound in order to clean it and accelerate its healing, they spat on a horse or cow in the belief that spirits and disease were kept away by the act.

The spittle of a fasting person was considered particularly efficacious, perhaps because it was felt to contain the undiluted essence of the person. In a less philosophical mood, people spat on money in the hope that it would become more plentiful!

Blood is what we are

The most essential of bodily elements is, of course, the blood. Because its spilling can cause death, and because it congeals at death, it was understood in many ancient cultures to contain the very spirit of life itself. Blood was considered synonymous with individuality, and so it was used as a guarantee in agreements and covenants; by signing in his own blood or by mixing it with that of another, the person committed himself totally.

Likewise, based on blood-lines, traits of character were thought to be hereditary or to 'run in families'. A person might be described as having a 'good drop' or a 'bad drop' in him if his actions were seen to be of a type with those of his ancestors.

The vein of poetry

The pulse, through which the 'life' of the blood

can most clearly be perceived, played an important role in these beliefs in Ireland. It was stressed in the case of poets, whose mystical skills were thought to reside in their own personalities.

The notion was prevalent that there was a special vein of poetry in a poet's body, a *féith na filíochta* which was not found in the bodies of other people. This vein was situated at the back of the head, a fancy which we can take to represent a primitive form of phrenology, but also perhaps to illustrate the 'hidden eye' of a genius. Gaelic poets, according to ancient ritual, composed in darkness, and the back of one's own head is an unseen, or 'dark', part of the body. When the poet began to compose, it was thought that the blood began to pulsate through this vein, and the metre of the poem corresponded to the pulsation.

Breeding breaks out

Events in one generation could, through their influence on the blood, have an effect for a long period afterwards. Thus, for instance, if a family were cursed, this could mean harm or misfortune in that family for seven generations. A curious element of this belief was that poetry, as an hereditary gift, would leave a family for seven generations if it manifested itself in a daughter rather than a son. This notion presumably owes something to the change of surname which would occur when the girl married. Poetry was, in late medieval Ireland, a profession specific to certain families — such as the O'Dalys, the Wards, the Keoghs, the Egans and the O'Higgins.

The importance of family

According to folk belief, the Keoghs shared a special attribute with those who had the surnames Cahill, Walsh, Darcy or Cassidy. This was that they could, by use of their blood, heal ringworm, wildfire and other ailments of the skin.

More generally, it was believed that cures could be performed by a person whose parents had the same surname, whatever that name might be. This belief probably derives from a fancy that the juncture of two streams of the same blood would bring out its inherent life-giving qualities in extraordinary relief. On a lighter note, children were told that if a boy and girl, at play, were injured and their blood intermingled, they were destined to marry when they grew up.

The pulse of life

The emphasis on blood as the life-force, flowing from the heart of the individual to the external organs, caused people to speculate that there was one vein or pulse on which all others depended. This was known as *cuisle na beatha* (the pulse of life). It was said that it might manifest itself in any part of the body, and that if it were struck a blow when seen to twitch or jump, the person would die. The old literature refers to this pulse as the *bradán* (salmon) of life, which warriors might eject from their bodies in the heat of combat, thereby expiring.

The belief persisted strongly in west Munster, where the *iasc* (fish) of life was spoken of as travelling around the body between the flesh and the skin. It was said to become obvious when one was under some form of strain, and resembled a nerve-quiver. Stories were told of how, due to a craving hunger or exhausting work, a particular person ejected this fish through his mouth, but a quick-witted companion seized it and prevailed on him to swallow it again, thus saving his life.

Crying out to heaven for justice

A belief commonly held abroad as in Ireland was that blood, since it belonged to the essence of a person, could bear witness of its loyalty to that person even after death. It was said, for instance, that the body of a murdered person would shed blood when the murderer came near to it, so exposing him. Another prevalent belief was that grass would not grow on the spot of earth where the blood of a slain person fell, or conversely that a fine tree would grow from that spot in honour of the dead.

The throbbing heart

The heart was generally understood as the source
of the emotions, even though these were structured
or rationalised in the head. Both feelings of
affection and feelings of revulsion and dislike were
believed to originate in the heart, which was said to
shake with fear and anger in reaction to hostile
circumstances. Emotions were stressed by saying
that they came from *lár an chroí* (the centre of the
heart), or sometimes even from the liver
underneath it. Thus, a common expression of
affection in Irish was *a chara na n-ae istigh*
(literally, o friend of the liver inside).

Since the heart was accorded such importance
in human behaviour, blood circulating to the limbs
was believed to carry instructions from it. This idea
was reinforced in popular lore by old medical
theories concerning the importance of particular
veins, such as the cephalic, which was in medieval
times thought to be the special conveyor of
messages from the heart to the limbs.

The hand which humanises

Information could be imparted manually in more
ways than one. The 'life-line', or fold at the base of
the thumb, in both ancient and modern times gave
rise to many fanciful interpretations. If long, it is said
to indicate deftness and skill; if deep and unbroken,

it portends a long life; and if crossed by several other lines, it suggests that one's life will be a varied and eventful one. The hand being the most industrious part of the body, it was employed symbolically in communications and in commerce. Waving, gesticulating and shaking hands are instances of this, and at markets, an Irish person would stress his commitment to a bargain by spitting on his palm before the concluding handshake.

The 'little men' at work

Each finger had its own name, and there was a tendency to attribute specific properties to them. To have an index finger of the same length as the third finger was in several countries considered a sinister sign, and in Ireland it was taken to indicate a stern or cruel nature, or alternatively a propensity for stealing. There was also a belief in many countries that a special vein runs from the heart to the third finger on the left hand, and in this way was explained the custom of wearing a wedding-ring on that finger. Another fancy was that the long finger on the right hand had a conduit to the life-centre, and a drop of blood pricked from it could cure the skin ailment wildfire.

The thumb was particularly valued, for it was thought to contain a cure for erysipelas and warts. Spittle was put on it, and it was then applied to the affected part. For a nose-bleed, a string was tied around the little finger on the same side as the affected nostril, the idea apparently being that the blocking of the blood-flow at one extremity of the hand would cause a similar blocking at the extremity of the face.

The fingers as signposts

A general custom, based on Christian imagery, was for the fingers to be crossed when danger of any type threatened. To look at a person from behind the extended fingers was believed to bring him bad luck, perhaps because this concentrated a hostile glance and made its destructive power more lethal. Death was thought to be presaged by a tingling or numbness in the fingers, or by the appearance of yellow or black marks on the nails. A less startling interpretation was given to white nail-marks, supposedly an indication that one would soon be undertaking a journey on the sea.

Nails, the essence externalised

The nails were regarded as an intrinsic part of an individual, since they grew from within. Discarded nails, like discarded hair, could be used by a hostile neighbour to do magical harm to a person — for instance, by burning them to cause painful and dangerous illnesses. This seems to have been the basis for the custom — general throughout Ireland

— of not cutting a baby's nails until he was twelve months old and therefore past the most vulnerable phase of his young life.

A play of folk fancy upon the Book of Genesis gave rise to a curious little idea. This was that the nails, along with the eyelashes, are the remains of the angelic covering (called *scéimh aingli*) which Adam and Eve had before their fall in the Garden of Eden. The presumption was that this covering would be restored to mankind after the General Judgment. The larynx in the throat was also widely believed to be an inheritance from the same Garden, for Adam — having accepted the apple from Eve — was said to have hesitated. He did not swallow the apple, and so it remained in his throat and in the throats of his descendants!

The biting edge of the body

Like the hair and nails, some people feared that teeth might be missing when the body was resurrected, and so they kept by them ones which had fallen out or had been extracted. Others, with more immediate concerns, worried when a tooth fell out that they would lose the remainder in a similar manner. So, all over Ireland, it was advised that such a tooth should be caught in the right hand and thrown backwards over the left shoulder, which it was claimed would prevent the precipitate loss of more. Another superstition was that a dream of losing a tooth presaged the death of oneself or of a close friend. In this case, the tooth seems to have been considered symbolical of the life-force or soul.

Voice, face, character and ambition

Other beliefs were derived from simple observation, coloured by a metaphoric tendency. Thus, a gap between the two front teeth is still commonly regarded as an indication that a person has a good singing voice, just as a wide mouth is thought to denote strength in such a voice. A thin mouth is, rather peremptorily, taken to signify stinginess and selfishness of character, and pinched cheeks are often given a similar interpretation. A prominent and pointed chin is humorously dubbed a symptom of forwardness or curiosity.

The skin feels and anticipates

As the outer layer of the body, the skin was thought to register what was in store from the external world, and various interpretations — some playful — attached to itchings on different parts of the body. Such a sensation on the palms of the hands was often said to indicate that one would before long be the recipient of a letter through the post or, better still, of money; though others interpreted 'itching of the palm' as an uncontrollable desire to spend money. Itching on the knuckles was a sign that one would soon be fighting, on the temples that one would soon have cause to weep, and on the eyebrows that one would soon be drinking whiskey. If a man's nose became itchy, it was said to presage a quarrel with his wife.

Strange marks, strange reality

Finally, marks on the skin were regarded as portents of special significance. A black or brown mark appearing overnight on the arm was thought to result from a pinch by a dead relative, indicating that one would soon be joining that relative in the afterlife. An ordinary mole on the skin was, however, considered a sign of health, and on the face of a young person was thought to enhance good looks.

In former centuries, Irish people, like people of other European countries, considered a red birthmark on the hand or arm of a political or military leader as a presage of remarkable achievements. Particularly dramatic was the notion that a Messianic leader would be born with the outline of a little red cross on his shoulder-blades. The noble O'Donnell family of Donegal believed for centuries that a great hero would come of their line and that he would be known as Aodh Balldearg (Hugh Red-spot).

Perhaps the most dramatic skin-mark in Irish tradition was that on the forehead of the mythical hero Diarmaid Ó Duibhne. It was bright and lustrous, and any woman who saw this *ball seirce* (love-spot) fell hopelessly in love with the young warrior. As one can well imagine, it became as much of a hindrance as a help to Diarmaid, and so he found it necessary to wear his war-helmet low down over his forehead even when not going into battle! Folklore claims that when the lady Gráinne, betrothed to Diarmaid's leader Fionn Mac Cumhaill, saw the *ball seirce*, she insisted that he elope with her. Fionn never forgave Diarmaid for this, and through his scheming, caused him to fight the vicious boar of Benbulben, in which titanic tussle the handsome young hero was slain.

TWO

THE WORLD AROUND US

*C*ulture, basically, is the way in which people
react to their surroundings. It is therefore not
surprising that such strong human feelings as curiosity
and fear tend to focus on aspects of the environment
which are continually, or repeatedly, encountered.
When there is a degree of mystery involved, the feeling
is increased. As a result, people developed many
superstitions concerning the environment; these in
time became stabilised as beliefs and are preserved
in folk tradition.

Great house of the world

The sky, massive and strange, was one of the
principal puzzles confronting the mind of man.
The mythologies of ancient peoples bear witness to
this in many different ways. Here in Ireland, the
sky was imagined as a kind of roof covering the
earth, as is clear from common expressions in the
Irish language such as *frathacha na firmiminte* (the
rafters of the firmament), *stua ceatha* (shower-arch,
meaning the rainbow) and *cranna na spéire* (the
columns of the sky). The sky-roof was, in medieval
times, thought to be held up by four huge columns

which stood outside the known realms of geography.

To the early Irish saints, earth and sky was one immense construction which reflected the architectural genius of God, 'the beloved smith who built that object, the god of heaven, he is the thatcher who roofed it'. This meant, of course, that there was something outside the sky, the great other-world beyond. One traditional saying describes the stars as 'pin-holes in the heavens, allowing the light out'.

There was therefore a respected basis for speculation that the constellations might have a connection with events which take place on the earth below. The antiquity of the practice of astrology in Ireland is unclear. The Celtic druids were claimed to have detailed knowledge of the moon and stars, and they certainly had developed a sophisticated calendar, but they seem to have made prognostications from the formations of the clouds rather than from the heavenly bodies.

Horseman of the heavens

Old Irish literature portrays the sun as a deity who traversed the heavens, a god who drove a fiery chariot, and this status is confirmed by the importance accorded to it in folk belief — where, indeed, it was often referred to as if it were a personage on high. Thus, in Irish the sun is described as going to lie down in the evening, or even going 'into its chair', and the long rays seen before dusk were referred to as 'the legs of the sun'. If affairs were going well with a person, he was said to be 'on the wheels of the sun', and it was a general practice for fishermen to turn their boats sun-wise when setting out to sea. Similarly, hay and corn stacks were constructed 'with the sun' — that is, by working the binding in the same direction as the sun crosses the sky. Even cures were applied with the intention of imitating the sun's course.

Health, wealth and inspiration

The sun, we are told sensibly enough, is 'the clothes of the poor', and it was said that if a person turned his clothes inside out at sunset, he would have luck. If the last of the sun contained precious energy, so, it was thought, must its beginning, and people used to wash their faces in sundew in early morning for health or to improve their complexions. Indeed, according to an old Irish text, sundew is 'a drop impregnated by the sun, and whoever consumes it gains the gift of poetry'.

The fact that the sun is the source of energy on earth could, of course, be guessed at from observation, even in a pre-scientific age. Its importance to the growth of crops and the strengthening of animals is evident. A common saying, 'Happy is the bride whom the sun shines on', meant that she would have a happy married life and be blessed with offspring. It was even believed that a woman would more easily conceive if she lay down for a while in the sunshine.

The eye of divine witness

The ancient pagan Irish adored the sun, a fact recorded by the early Christian writers here. According to these writers, the Irish swore oaths by the heavenly bodies, and such an expression survives in the Irish language — *dar brí na gréine is na gealaí* (by the strength of the sun and of the moon). Early Christianity, aware of the importance attributed by the Romans and others to midwinter, when the sun was 'reborn', decided to celebrate the birth of the Saviour at that time, and thus 25 December was settled upon as Christmas.

The dancing fire

The appropriation of the sun as an image of Christ, 'the true light of the world', persisted to medieval times, when a superstition spread throughout Europe that on Easter morning the sun danced in the sky with joy at the Resurrection. The sun's image does indeed shimmer on many spring mornings due to the mingling of hot and cold air at the earth's surface. The belief was very strong in Ireland, with people climbing to hilltops to witness the dancing sun as Easter dawned. It was common also to watch the reflection of the Easter morning sun in a well or in a tub of water.

The sun lives and dies

A curious belief was that the sun could quench the household fire if the latter were exposed to it, because sunlight seems to diminish the light of fire. It was also supposed that sunlight took the edges off knives and scythes, and this 'biting' potential is further instanced by references to butter which melted on a fine summer's day as having been eaten by the sun.

Given the long-standing recognition of our dependence on the sun, it is not surprising that an eclipse, even a partial one, caused consternation. People feared that the hand of destiny had smothered the sun, and for the duration of the eclipse they prayed that the Almighty might relent and allow it to shine again. As in many other cultures, a solar eclipse was taken as a sign of disaster to come. Such an eclipse in the year 1652 was believed to have presaged the massive confiscations of Irish land by the Cromwellian government, and the partial eclipse of 1846 — following on the near-total one of four years earlier — was remembered as a portent of the Great Famine.

The moon — maiden and hag

The heavenly body which is seen continually to undergo change was long an object of superstition. The ancient Celtic druids placed great emphasis on the moon, arranging their calendar by it, and believing that business undertaken while it was growing would be successful. This notion that human affairs depend on the waning and waxing of the moon persists in many countries. In Ireland, a child born when there was a new moon was thought to have especially good prospects for health and wealth, and attempts were even made to delay births until that time.

Growth and decay from above

The lunar conjunction was generally regarded as an unlucky time, as no moon was then visible and people felt that their good fortune had likewise departed, even if only temporarily. Seeds might, however, be sown in the earth at this time — as they would be concealed for a brief period corresponding to the moon's disappearance, would begin to sprout as the new moon emerged, and would grow copiously with it. Scollops for thatching the roof would be cut as the moon increased, thereby ensuring their continuing strength.

Conversely, any new undertakings would be avoided as much as possible during the waning of the moon — except in cases where loss was actually the desired object. An indirect benefit of the waning moon was that body-sores were believed to decrease in size during it, and warts might disappear altogether. Furthermore, farmers insisted on this time for the castration of their animals, as it was thought to leave the effect of that operation beyond doubt.

The killing of pigs and sheep was carefully arranged according to the same calculations. It was claimed that, if the slaughter took place while the moon was waxing, the bacon or mutton would 'swell in the boil'; if done while the moon was on the wane, it would 'shrink in the boil'. Needless to say, people were much more inclined to spare their money as the moon filled, and to spend it as the moon waned!

The eternal return

The coming of a new moon was naturally something of a mystery, and attracted much attention. 'On the first night nobody sees it, on the second night the birds see it, on the third night everybody sees it' — so goes an Irish saying. Its coming was not greeted without apprehension, and people were advised to make the Sign of the Cross when they first noticed it. A prayer might also be recited, such as 'God bless the moon and God bless me, I see the moon and the moon sees me.'

There was a strong and enduring country tradition that, with the coming of the new moon, people would kneel and pray in Irish for health, wealth and good fortune. A seventeenth-century German book remarks: 'The wild Irish have this custom, that when the moon is new they squat upon their knees and pray to the moon that it may leave them vigorous and healthy, as it has found them, and they request particularly that they may be safe from wolves.'

Minerals from the sky

It was considered lucky to look at the new moon through the clear air, but unlucky to see it through glass. This must derive from the general belief that the body's internal organism is affected by moonlight, a doctrine taught by the alchemists of the Middle Ages. The alchemists further claimed that various minerals were developed in the earth by different planets, the mineral which thus benefited from the moon being silver. A very common superstition was that, when the new moon appeared, a person should turn the money around in his pocket, the idea here seeming to be that a silver coin would flourish if both of its sides were exposed to the moon's rays. Notions about these rays are doubtless behind other beliefs, such as that a person should not look sideways at the moon, but should face it directly.

Potential and reproduction

The most obvious parallel between the moon and
human life is the comparable length of its cycle
and that of the menstrual cycle in women. As a
result, it was thought that women should not stare
at the moon, or discuss it in detail, for fear of
complications in menstruation. On the other hand,
the new moon provided a good occasion to make a
wish, and both men and women sought to avail of
this in matters of romance. And if one were to tie a
little bag of clay around the neck when going to
bed, it was said that one's future spouse would
appear in a dream.

The heave and pull

It was claimed in folklore that Aristotle failed to
gain an understanding of three things: 'the work of
the bees, the coming and going of the tide, and the
mind of a woman'! Whatever about the other two,
ordinary people understood that the tides had
some connection with the moon, and this provided
ready 'proof' of the ubiquitous lunar influences.

Contemplating the strange connection between
sea and moon, folklore developed some dramatic
ideas. One such was that all water reacts in the
same way as the sea; that rivers, for instance,
swelled with the full moon, or that water placed in
a dish will rise and overflow as the full moon is

seen to rise. At the same time, the blood becomes
invigorated and a person feels his strength increase.
The sap rising in the horns of a cow with the rising
moon was believed to cause the horns to soften,
allowing the owner to straighten them. Some
people even held that stones softened with the
rising moon, and that drops of perspiration could
be seen on them!

Shadows in the moonlight

The energy caused by the full moon in all its
strength could, it was thought, be overpowering to
the human spirit, and the belief was widespread in
Ireland and abroad that a person might become
over-elated by it and lose his wits entirely for a
while. Such a person was said to have gone *le
gealaigh* (with the moon). In English, indeed, the
word 'lunatic' and its synonym 'moonstruck' derive
from this very ancient belief. Even birds were
affected, it being said that they lived in dread of
their shadows at this time.

Folklore attempted to lessen the apprehension
concerning the full moon by claiming, logically
enough, that the moon was 'full' in a complete
sense for only a very short time, and that its effects
would gradually wear off afterwards. It was often
held that a full moon on Saturday betokened bad
weather or some other local misfortune. However,
those with a livelier and more bizarre imagination

claimed that if ever a Saturday full moon were to coincide exactly with the highest point of the tide, then the sea would rise and drown the whole world!

Man at the mercy of the unknown

Lore of the planets and stars was less alarming, though it too had its danger-points. For instance, the appearance of a 'tailed star', or comet, was often taken to presage some disaster. Due to the influence of medieval astrology, it was thought that each child was born under a particular planet. If that planet seemed relaxed and quiet at the birth, he would have a good life, while if it sparkled, the opposite would apply. Many stories were told of scholars and learned people trying to get women to delay giving birth until the opportune time!

One of the phenomena most noticed in the heavens was a meteor, or 'falling star', the general belief being that it represented the release of a soul from Purgatory into Heaven. It was customary to make the Sign of the Cross and utter a little prayer of thanks to God when such a 'star' was noticed. In a more secular vein, it was sometimes said that a wish made upon seeing a falling star would be granted.

A natural explanation was often given, to the effect that such a 'star' would hit the earth, and that frog-spawn or similar slimy substances seen on the ground in the morning were the remains of it.

Twinkle, twinkle, little star

These heavenly bodies were given a romantic
significance, as one might expect. It was often said
that if a young man or woman were to count nine
stars each night for nine consecutive nights, he or
she would meet the future spouse without delay.
All of this fanciful lore did not preclude more
rational use of the constellations, for purposes such
as navigating both on land and at sea. Most
important of all in this context was, of course, the
north star, called appropriately in Irish *an réalt
eolais* (the star of knowledge).

Clocks were not in general use in olden times,
and systems were therefore devised to read the time
from the heavens. For instance, the Pleiades (called
in Irish *an Tréidín*, or the little herd) were closely
observed, for the time of night could be read from
their position as they traversed the sky.

Who is there?

Traditional lore is a mosaic of realistic and fanciful
interpretations, and many of the fanciful elements
are quite humorous. Especially notable are the
personifications of natural phenomena. In many
countries, the markings on the moon are
interpreted as being the body of a man who was
transported there from the earth. Some Irish
versions of this belief claim that he was a thief who

stole a bush from his neighbours and was sent
there as a punishment, while others state that his
offence was to go to collect firewood on Sunday
when he should have been in church.

Gale force gathering

Perhaps it was the man in the moon who suggested
to people that there might also be a man in the
wind. He was known as *fear na gaoithe* (the wind-
man), and was said to go about in the late autumn
knocking the stacks of corn and hay which lazy
farmers had not yet gathered into the barn.
Alternatively, he was said to control and direct
storms, blowing them with a bellows.

A popular Munster story told of how a widow's
son, angry at damage done to his mother's house,
once set out to get satisfaction from the wind-man.
He followed the direction from which the wind
was blowing, until he reached its ultimate source
— a large hole in the ground, where he met the
wind-man and made his complaint. The wind-man
had not been aware of the damage he had done to
the widow, and as compensation presented the
youngster with a bellows which could control
storms. Through the use of his acquired gift, the
youngster grew up to be a very rich man.

Behind this humorous tale lie ancient attempts
to explain what caused the wind to blow. Many
early mythologies represented storms as resulting

from the anger of the gods or from their furious travelling through the air. Such an idea was current in Ireland also, the wind being explained as the moving about of the *sí*, the other-world beings known in English as the fairies.

Especially feared was a whirlwind, supposed to be the shock-troops of the fairies moving about. It was said that one should never look in its direction but should utter a prayer. The usual term for the phenomenon was *sitheadh gaoithe* (literally, thrust of wind), but this was pronounced almost identically with *sí gaoithe* (fairies of wind), which facilitated the supernatural identification. The whirlwind was sometimes also alluded to as *deamhain aeir* (literally, demons of the air), and reference to such frightful beings was circumvented by substituting as their name *leamhain aeir* (moths of the air). In the older literature, the swishing of weapons in battle was claimed to be the screeches of war-demons.

The wanderer through the world

A personage was also associated with the phenomenon known as ignus fatuus, the *tine ghealáin* or 'bright fire' seen over swampy land at night. This is said to be the soul of a master-gambler, who defeated the devil at cards but was refused entry into Heaven because of his profession. He therefore wanders interminably around the earth seeking a place to spend eternity and carrying a lantern which gives off the strange light. He is known in some localities as 'Jack of the Lantern', and in others as 'Will of the Wisp'.

The sky a witness to pain

Early Irish literature contains accounts of several personages who seem to have originated in sun-myths, such as the ancestor deity Eochaidh Aonsúile (One-eyed Horseman), and the infamous Balar of the Evil Eye, whose glance destroyed multitudes. There is little evidence for personification of the other heavenly bodies, but folklore commemorates the mythical cow who gave a near-inexhaustible supply of milk. She was known as the Glas Ghoibhneann (that is, the 'grey' of the smith-god Goibhniu). A malicious woman once bet her owner that there was one vessel which the great cow could not fill, and then put a sieve under her. The reliable Glas died trying to fill the sieve, but her effort was so massive, and so copiously did the milk flow from her, that it spurted up to the heavens and coloured an immense cluster of stars. This is the Milky Way!

Mysteries of the deep

The sea too was personified, with a mysterious old man said to control the waters of the deep. When

God created the world, he told this man to be careful not to allow anybody to drown, but the man disobeyed these instructions and regularly demands the lives of people as tribute: hence the fatalistic saying, *Bíonn a cuid féin ag an bhfarraige* (The sea must have its due). It was considered unlucky to save a drowning person, for the sea would in time take the rescuer as compensation for its loss of tribute.

According to a story told in Ireland and abroad to explain why sea-water was salty, a ship's captain once got possession of a little magical mill which ground salt. The captain was transporting the mill in his ship, but he was an impatient fellow and could not wait to reach land before testing it. He therefore set it to work, but forgot the word which would make it cease. The weight of salt which the mill produced caused the ship to sink, and ever since it churns out salt from the bottom of the deep.

The mighty pounding heart

Movement of the sea, what could be perceived as its living vigour, is expressed by each wave (in Irish, *tonn*). Fairies of the sea were said to travel in certain waves, which could thus be made to subside by throwing a knife or some other weapon at them. One common story told of a man who in this way injured the eye of a fairy lady, and was afterwards brought to 'the world under the sea' in order to remove the offending weapon. The ninth wave out from the shore is represented, in the old literature and in later folklore, as a particularly dangerous one. It was known as the *tonn bháite*, or 'drowning wave'.

No doubt on account of other-world beings residing in the waves, the ancient Irish poets were believed to be able to interpret what their voices were saying. There was a very old tradition that the sea around Ireland had four great waves, which cried out to foretell a catastrophe, such as the death of a king. Two of these waves were off the south-west coast — Tonn Chlíona (in Tralee Bay) and Tonn Tóime (in Kenmare Bay). The other two were off the north-east coast — Tonn Tuaidhe (in Rathlin Sound) and Tonn Ruaidhrighe (in Dundrum Bay).

Voices from the beyond

Speculation concerning unusual or notable sounds was very common. Thunder was explained as the angels in Heaven performing drill, while lightning was the flashing of their swords. A fanciful little explanation for echoes was that they were the voices of souls in distress. It was thought that, for some souls, Purgatory could be spent within the natural landscape, such as in a thorny bush, under the leaf of a tree, or between the froth and the river.

Perhaps older is the interpretation of echoes as the speech of fairies, and in hills and rocky places questions were put to fairies in the expectation of some decipherable reply. A more rational, if un-scientific, explanation was that an echo was caused by the sound striking against underground water.

Deeds in water writ

Water has long been associated with the other-world. Almost all the rivers of Ireland have female names, and the old literature depicts other-world women as presiding over them. The original mythical idea seems to have been that both land and river represented the body of the tutelary goddess. Little of this survives in folklore, except that spirits and fairies were often encountered on the banks of rivers and lakes.

Water, as an element essential to life, was a favourite abode of the old Celtic gods, and there was a feeling that all types of water were in communion with each other. This is graphically portrayed in a medieval belief that an inland well at Kesh in Co. Sligo had a correspondence with the sea, draining and filling according as the tide ebbed and flowed far away.

The cleansing power

The veneration of holy wells, general throughout Ireland down to recent times, is a good example of how the ancient tradition of gods residing in water was adopted into Christian practice. People congregated at these wells, each of which was dedicated to a particular saint, on the feast-day of that saint. Many of the wells were thought to contain cures for specific ailments, a common belief being that, if a cure were to be effected, a little white fish would be seen in the water.

It was frequently said that a holy well had moved from one position to another — across a road, for instance — because somebody had fouled it, a piece of lore which developed to explain the fact that underground water can vary its point of emergence to the surface.

The brink of disaster

The fear of drowning loomed large in the case of rivers and lakes as well as in the case of the sea. It was said that someone was drowned once every seven years in particular rivers or lakes, and it was even told of some rivers that a voice would be heard periodically crying out and claiming its sinister due: *Anois an t-am, cá bhfuil an duine?* (Now is the time, where is the person?)

More pleasant was the belief that fine horses and cattle could come from a lake, or even from the sea, and mix with ordinary stock. This lore was especially strong as regards horses, and many accounts were given of how a farmer would notice a strange stallion in his fields by a lakeside. The stallion might turn out to be a great workhorse or even racer, and the farmer could breed some splendid stock from it. Usually, however, it was said that the farmer on some occasion lost his temper with the animal and struck it, after which it returned to the lake. Some grisly details might be added, such as that the farmer swam into the lake to recover it but was savaged by the horse, and pieces of his body were afterwards seen floating on the water.

In order to explain how strange beings might come from the water, extensive use was made of the idea that some ancient city had been inundated and had sunk to the bottom of the sea or of a lake. Thus, folklore claimed that fishermen often heard the sound of music or of bells coming from under the water; and luminous reflections on the surface were claimed to be street-lamps far below.

Far over the sea

A much older idea — stretching back to the pre-Christian religion of the Celts — was that the other-world was situated on a lonely island in the sea. It was anciently called *Magh Meall* (the Plain of Delight), and also *Tír na hÓige* (the Land of Youth) or *Tír na nÓg* (meaning the land whose inhabitants remain ever-young). Under Christian influence, it became known as *Tír Tairngire* (the Land of Promise). Following the same pattern, folklore claims that there is an other-world island off the west coast called *Uí Bhreasaíl*, and sun-rays reflected far away on the sea are pointed out to children as this island. More prevalent was the belief that *Uí Bhreasaíl* was under the water and surfaced only at specific times.

Various names were given in coastal areas to this other-world island. In Co. Clare, it was called *Cill Stoithín* — probably a corruption of Cill Scoithín, meaning the church of Scoithín, who is mentioned in early Irish literature as a celebrated seafaring saint. This island is surrounded by a magical mist, which lifts once every seven years, at which time it can be reached by boat. It is said that the island can be disenchanted by unlocking the door of a fine building which lies there, but the key is hidden in a lake on top of a mainland mountain.

Intruders on solitude

Water-horses and water-cattle were usually interpreted as belonging to those fairies who inhabited the aquatic realms. Fairies on land had their own livestock — or if not, were intent on gaining some. As a result, people were anxious when sending their cattle to lonely pastures, for fear they might be 'elf-shot': that is, that the fairies would hit the animals with darts which would cause them to pine away and die and thus be acquired by the farmers of fairyland. Little chips of stone found on the ground — some, in fact, remains of ancient arrowheads — were suspected of being such 'fairy-darts'.

Special care was taken when sending cattle to graze near bogs or on hills, where the fairies were very numerous — for example, the cattle might be struck with a hazel-rod or a branch of the rowan-tree for protection, or blessed with the Sign of the Cross. Fairy-lore is often very close to lore of the dead, and the idea that fairies resided underneath bogs or within mounds and hilltop cairns may be a survival from ancient burial customs.

It should be remarked that, while the association of eeriness or sacredness with lonely locations was intermittent rather than general in Irish culture, it does seem to be a relic of antiquity. For instance, although cases of butter were buried in bogs for purposes of preservation down to recent centuries, this manner of butter-burying seems originally to have represented an offering to placate the spirits of the bogs. A related practice which survived until lately was to throw the first measure into the air at milking-time as an offering to the fairies.

Mysteries underground

Indentations in the landscape have long attracted attention and suspicion. The great prehistoric caverns — at Dunmore in Co. Kilkenny, Aillwee in

Co. Clare and Mitchelstown in Co. Cork — were anciently known as 'the three dark places of Ireland'. That at Dunmore was, indeed, said to have been inhabited by a monstrous cat, and a drove of such creatures was reputed to have resided in a cave at Rathcroghan in Co. Roscommon. The most famous of all sinister caverns was on an island in Lough Derg in Co. Donegal, called 'St Patrick's Purgatory', which was in the Middle Ages claimed to be the mouth of Hell itself!

More benign was the folk belief that under-ground passages linked many of the raths and tumuli of Ireland. This belief, which is still very strong, was based on the use in olden times of souterrains, or dug-out caves, for storing food. People have speculated that these were the openings of interconnected tunnels constructed by the *Tuatha Dé Danann*, a magical race which lived underground. Many folk traditions claim that these tunnels were later used by the Irish for purposes of escape from the Elizabethan and Cromwellian armies.

Surveying all

The custom of climbing hills and mountains at certain festivals is of great antiquity and has not yet died out. The old literature contains several suggestions that communication with the other-world took place at lofty locations — the most celebrated instance being the Hill of Tara in Co. Meath, which from time immemorial was regarded as a sacred site. That hill's name, *Teamhair*, meant 'Spectacle', witness to the fine view it afforded mortals and gods over a broad stretch of the midlands. In an aesthetic sense, Irish tradition claims that poets could find inspiration on hilltops. Due to the force of gravity, proclamations made from such locations were thought to have particular impact.

The landscape protests

The combined mystical and menacing nature of
lonely places caused them often to be regarded
with a degree of awe. The most striking instance of
this attitude in folklore concerns the *féar gortach*
(hungry grass), described as an unlucky patch
which may grow in isolated parts of mountainsides.
If a traveller were to step on this grass, he would
grow weaker and weaker from hunger, and would
die unless some remedy were in store. People
therefore took the precaution of bringing a piece of
bread with them when going on long journeys, as
this was thought to counter the magical effect of
the hungry grass. This is a simple example of the
spiritualising of a very important practice in
normal life — that of bringing food for a journey
— but there may also be in its background an
element of food-offering to the spirits of the wild.

Another unforeseen hazard of the countryside
was called the *fóidín mearbhaill* or 'wayward sod',
which, if trodden upon, would set a person astray.
Most accounts of this have the mishap occurring at
night, with the result that the traveller would cover
long distances and continually end up at the same
spot, until the light of day brought deliverance.
Here again is a dramatic expression of a real
dilemma, as losing the way in unfamiliar
surroundings often leaves one travelling in circles.

Man astray in the world

Another exaggeration of reality was the fairy mist,
known in Irish as *ceo draíochta*, which also puts a
person astray until he finds his bearings. This mist
can descend suddenly and without warning,
usually at night and in remote places, and it was
sometimes said to be a portent of one's impending
death. In the old literature, the descent of
such a mist was a preliminary to an adventure in
fairyland, underlining the idea that unfamiliar
surroundings can be the juncture between the
ordinary world and the other-world.

Tree of the world

Of trees, the rowan, called in Irish *caorthann* and
in Hiberno-English 'mountain ash', was considered
the luckiest species and the most effective against
fairy interference. A branch of the rowan was often
kept in the cow-byre, so as to ensure a good milk-
yield, and might also be kept in the dwelling-house
in the belief that it prevented fire. The *sceach gheal*
or whitethorn, on the other hand, was the tree
most associated with the fairies, and would never
be brought into a building.

The general reluctance to cut down trees,
except for some very good purpose, stems from the
veneration of them in ancient Ireland. The old
literature, indeed, speaks of many a great old tree

(called *bile*), which acted as a kind of protector of the landscape. This idea seems to be based on the sheltering function of a tree, and perhaps also on the notion that the sky was held up on columns. Most notable of all was the *Bile Tartain* (at Ardbraccan in Co. Meath), which was an ash of gigantic size said to have existed since the beginning of the world.

THREE

OURSELVES AND THE OTHERS

*R*ealising that the human race shared the world
with many kinds of creatures, and sensing that
different forms of life were interdependent, people
were curious about the identity and purpose of these
other creatures, and there are a lot of old traditions
concerning the various species of fauna. Very prevalent
was the idea that they could congregate for their
mutual benefit, just as humans did. Many countries
have folktales telling of parliaments convened by the
animals and birds. The quadrupeds chose the lion as
their king, and the birds would have elected the eagle
but for the fact that the wren hid in its tail and
thereby flew higher, gaining the crown for itself.

Such a fanciful way of thinking gave rise to
many superstitions, most notably that some species
were originally human but had been enchanted
long ago into their present forms. This, to the self-
centred human mind, made the secrets of nature
more comprehensible, but folk imagination did
not stop there. The many puzzling features of the
world, and the many unexplained occurrences, led
to the idea that the earth was inhabited also by
mystical beings, such as spirits and fairies, which
were as real as the more obvious physical beings.

The extended nostrils

Since they were in closest proximity to people, superstitions abounded concerning domestic animals, their natures and habits. It was generally believed that horses had the power to see spirits, and that they would stop on the road at haunted places and could not be persuaded to move on. This fancy seems to be based on observation of the natural skittishness of horses and of their very keen sense of smell, both of which cause them to balk at anything they find threatening. Folklore claimed that if a rider or carter looked ahead directly between the horse's ears on such an occasion, he would be able to see the spirit which was there.

Danger to property

Horses were of great importance in the business and social life of long ago, and people were very anxious lest any mishap befall them. So there was a wide range of beliefs as to how a malicious person might do harm to a neighbour's horse by envious praise or by use of the evil eye. Possible interference by the fairies, too, was feared, and so it was usual for an owner to spit on his horse both morning and night, for the fairies were quite fastidious and would have nothing to do with anything which had been soiled. It was also said that the horse sneezed in order to protect itself from the fairies.

One type of horse was well able to defend itself, if folklore is to be credited. This was the *fíorláir* (true mare), defined as being the seventh filly born to its dam without any colt intervening. Such mares were considered unusually good workers and gallopers, and neither magic nor spirits had any effect on them. Indeed, stories were told of how they could protect their owners from malice and misfortune. It was said that where the true mare was dropped by its dam at birth, the four-leaved shamrock grew. This was known as the *Seamair Mhuire* (the Virgin Mary's Clover) and was much in demand as a talisman.

The blessed horse

Horses were often said to be lucky animals, and people got them to trample a little on newly sown fields, as this would cause the seeds to sprout well. The horse's halter was believed to bring good luck, and was always kept by the seller when the animal was sold. The value or good fortune of the animal, which had been enclosed by the halter, would be retained within that trapping.

The cow is leather, meat and milk

Cattle were, of course, also of great value, and this fact too was projected onto the other-world. Their owners feared that the fairies would try to take the cattle, and objects considered repugnant to the fairies were attached to them. A favourite method was to tie a rowan-twig to the tail of a cow, or to rub dung on her udder. Another common trick was to have the cow inhale smoke, which, it was believed, other-world beings could not tolerate. However, cracks in a cow's skin were thought to be caused by fairy darts, and to be a preliminary to her health fading away.

Cows without horns were said to be good milkers, as it was believed that horns sapped up the energy of an animal. Since music was thought to increase cows' yield, people often sang or whistled while milking. A curious tradition attached to the keeping of bulls. It was said that the animal should never be placed in a field where an echo could be heard, because, on hearing his lowing repeated, he would think that another bull was present, would be constantly restive and would pine away.

Goats and donkeys

Goats are noticeably quick to seek shelter when they sense the approach of rain, which gave rise to the belief that they could see the wind. Probably also because of this, as well as the fact that it can eat many noxious weeds, the goat was thought of as a sort of guardian-animal, and was believed to bring luck to a farm. A billy-goat (*pocán*) was often put among the cattle herd, in the belief that its presence prevented cows from aborting and increased their milk yield. The donkey was also considered a lucky animal, and one deserving of special kindness, because of the widespread belief that it got the cross on its back when it carried Christ long ago.

Pecking about for clues

Because of the importance of the egg supply, much lore centred on hens. There is an old saying, 'A whistling woman or a crowing hen bodes no good for God or men!' The crowing, like the whistling, was supposed to be a male trait, meaning that the hen might not produce many eggs, and would be unlucky in a farmyard.

Bad luck was also believed to attach to a white cock, probably because it was the opposite to an all-black one, which was thought to provide protection against danger from all unexpected sources. The black cock crowed to banish spirits, and if hatched in March had especially strong protective power. A common folk legend told of how a seaman once purchased such a 'March cock' from a farmhouse near the shore. As soon as he had taken the bird away, a thunderbolt struck the house.

Hidden hostility

It was claimed that hens had been brought here by the Vikings, and that they had hostile feelings towards the Irish people. This was what caused them continually to scrape on the kitchen floor, in an attempt to set the house on fire. They made preparations each night to return to Scandinavia, but in the morning forgot all their plans! Other animals said to have been brought as pets to Ireland by the Vikings included foxes, which were their dogs, and stoats, which were their cats.

Friends and foes

It is said that the dog and the cat argued long ago over which of them would have first claim on the shelter of the house. They decided to wager the matter on a race towards the building. The dog was winning but stopped to attack a beggar and lost, so the cat ever since has choice position next to the family fire.

There were, indeed, many superstitions concerning these household animals. The dog is man's best friend but, because of its fierce nature, should not be fully trusted. Therefore, it was said that one should never ask a question of a dog, lest it answer back. Cats were much valued for their services against rats and mice, but were believed to have a secret nature of their own, far removed from that of people. This springs from observation of the nocturnal life of cats, and of their ability to see in the dark. It was said that even the household cat dreams three times each night of killing its owners, and is deterred from doing so only by fear of the household dog.

Creatures of the night

A story was told in Ireland and in other European countries of a man who, returning from the market, was attacked by a cat. He slew the animal, but before it expired, it spoke and told him to let the other cats know what had happened. When he reached home and was telling his wife of this, the household cat jumped up and attempted to tear at his throat. It transpired that the dead animal had been the king of the cats.

Other tales told of how the cats held nocturnal assemblies, where they discussed their affairs, and where humans who eavesdropped might be savagely attacked. It was believed that cats were very vengeful, and that even quiet domestic cats consorted with their wild cousins. Wild cats, formerly common in lonely parts of the country, were said to be vicious fighters and easily to get the upper hand of dogs. A wild cat, it was said, had a claw in its tail, which it used to deadly effect in fights.

Tally-ho

Of the wild animals, pride of place in storytelling went to the fox, which was celebrated for its cleverness in preying on farmyard fowl and in evading capture. Due to its red colour, which suggested blood-spilling, it was thought to be an unlucky animal to behold when one was beginning some enterprise. Fishermen dreaded to mention the word 'fox' when at sea, probably also because it was felt that so conspicuous a land-animal was inappropriate to that context.

A superstition attaching to some wealthy families — such as the Prestons and the Frenches — was that foxes congregated about their houses, barking mournfully, when a member of these families was about to die.

The sleepless king

The otter was the subject of much fancy. Because of its peculiar eye-folds, it was thought to sleep with its eyes open. One special type, known as the 'king-otter', was said never to sleep. This king-otter had a rare coloration, much of its body being white, but with a cross on its back and its paws and ears black. It was thought very difficult to kill one, except with a silver bullet, and there was a belief that the person who killed it would not live long afterwards.

Possession of the pelt of a king-otter guaranteed immunity from danger. In general, it was said that any otter, if attacked, would put his tail in his mouth and whistle, thus attracting other otters to his assistance.

People of the sea

The seals were popularly claimed to be descendants of the people left outside Noah's ark, who on rare occasions cast aside their seal-skins and danced on the shore in human shape. A story was told in some coastal areas of how a man once gained possession of the skin of a seal-woman, and while he held that she remained in human form. She married him, but on finding her skin one day, returned to the deep. This human nature attributed to seals probably derived from the human-like cry sometimes heard from these animals. Indeed, versions of the legend above bring the seal-woman nearer to human shape by calling her a mermaid.

Little suspicions

The Irish stoat (*easóg*) is usually referred to in Hiberno-English as a 'weasel'. These animals are also thought to have human characteristics, organising their affairs communally and even holding funerals for their dead. To meet a weasel when setting out on a journey was a bad portent, but one could avoid the bad luck by enquiring after its health and addressing it as *a bheainín bheag uasal* (o little noble woman). Its spit was believed to be poisonous, but it was not a hostile animal unless provoked. Once, we are told, a group of haymakers accidentally destroyed a weasel's nest and, on seeing this, the mother-weasel spat in their tea-can. One of the men, however, put the young creatures in a safe place, whereupon the mother came and deliberately knocked over the can so that the men would not be poisoned.

For some reason, weasels were often said to steal coins and hoard them, and therefore it was thought that a purse made from the skin of this animal would bring wealth to its possessor. On the other hand, to take money from its nest, or otherwise to upset it, would bring bad luck. A story was told in different parts of Ireland about a man who interfered with the nest of a weasel, which came after him for revenge. In a desperate attempt to escape his pursuer, the man took ship to a foreign country, but the vengeful animal followed him on board. It traced him all the way to his new dwelling, and would have seized him by the throat while he slept had not a friend come to his assistance.

Wildest of all

Throughout most of Europe and further afield, the hare was traditionally regarded as an unlucky and even sinister creature. This idea is probably due to its nervousness and wildness, which caused man to associate it with the insecure and unknown side of his own nature. The Irish word for a hare (*giorria*) originally meant 'little wild one', or even 'little deer'. Because it lived in the wilderness and avoided humans, the ancient Irish regarded the deer as a strange animal which consorted with other-world beings, and they saw the hare in a similar light. Even in late folklore, it is said that fairies can take the form of hares, an all-white hare being especially suspect.

More disturbing notions, such as that it was unlucky to see a hare early in the morning, or that a hare lurking near the house was a sign that a member of the family was going to die, seem to have come into this country in the Middle Ages. Likewise the idea that some old women could transform themselves into the shape of a hare, which was one of the beliefs concerning witches in medieval Europe. A story is commonly told in Ireland of a farmer who noticed that the milk yield had fallen, and early one morning found a hare drinking from the cows. He attacked and wounded the hare, but it escaped, and while chasing it he came to a house where an old lady lived. He saw that she was bleeding and confronted her with this, upon which she turned back into a hare, and was killed by his dogs.

Furry mysteries

A more friendly view was held of the rabbit, as its meat was eaten and its skin used in the making of caps. Care was, however, taken in killing the animals, as dead friends and relatives were thought to return in this form on occasions to spend some time near their former dwellings.

Mice, on the other hand, ate the family food and were therefore not so welcome. They were, of course, especially busy at night, and a sore spot on the lips might be referred to as *mún luchóige* (mouse urine), in the belief that some mouse had relieved itself on the mouth of the sleeping person. On the more positive side, it was said that to eat the soup of a mouse could endow a person with the ability to see hidden treasure!

Protecting the food

The rat was the greatest pest in Irish life, as it ate and dirtied the grain. Accordingly, there was a wide range of superstitions deprecating it. The rat was introduced to Ireland from Norman ships in medieval times, and so, while in most areas it was called simply *luch mhór* (big mouse), in southern

dialects its designation was *francach* (literally, the French one).

Folklore explained that both mice and rats originated when St Martin of Tours was salting bacon in an upturned tub. A curious woman, despite the saint's protestations, lifted the tub, and immediately the rodents raced out. Realising what a plague to humanity these creatures would be, Martin flung his glove after them, and the glove turned into a cat — hence the very first feline creature!

The triumph of verse

Since a rat's bite can be poisonous, these creatures were thought to be very vengeful and dangerous. They were also quite audacious, and one lurid tradition is that they sometimes came and drank from the breasts of sleeping women. According to a curious Irish belief, both rats and mice obey orders given to them in verse, and it was even thought that they would follow poetic instructions which were written on a piece of paper and left in a place frequented by them.

The power which Gaelic poets were said to have over rats caused some amazement to their English counterparts, and references to it are found in the works of William Shakespeare, Ben Jonson and others. Folklore records how a family whose house or barn was infested with rats would send for the local poet and have him rhyme them away. One had to be careful, however, for poets could direct the rats to go elsewhere, and a person whose pomposity or stinginess had incurred a poet's displeasure could find such a misfortune inflicted on him.

Rats were said in this way to be 'billeted' on somebody, and there were many descriptions of a mighty drove of the creatures travelling along the road under poetic orders to move from one place to another. The drove was usually led by an old decrepit rat, the senior of his clan, who would be leaning on a stick suspended between the mouths of two younger and stronger rats!

Unpleasant company and sinking ships

A rather different suggestion was that rats could bring luck to a place, provided that their numbers were kept within reason. Since these creatures are filthy and dangerous to food, and since it is very difficult completely to rid a place of them, this may have been invented in order to console people. A similar attempt to provide consolation is found in the frequent assertion that to tread accidentally in excrement is a sign of good luck.

The strong belief that the presence of rats on a ship is lucky has, however, a more realistic basis. It is well known, and often asserted as a proverb, that a vessel in danger of foundering is quickly deserted by these creatures, and so their presence on board could be taken to indicate that all was well.

Fate on the wing

The ancient Celts considered the raven to be a significant bird of augury, and its flight was carefully noted in the belief that the future could be divined from it. It is generally seen in negative terms. For example, the appearance of a raven while new work is being undertaken signifies that the work will not be a success; near the dwelling-house, it is taken as an omen that some member of the household will soon die. Crows are also portentous, but in their case it is thought unlucky if they leave the house or farm.

The most unlucky of all birds to see is the magpie. This belief must derive from its unusual colouring, the starkly contrasting black and white which is very noticeable and therefore felt to be unnatural. Likewise, to meet with a speckled horse — called a 'magpie pony' — is often considered a bad omen. It was thought, in fact, that the magpie was not a natural inhabitant of the Irish landscape at all, but had been brought here by Cromwell's soldiers.

A more welcome introduction, if folklore is to be credited, was the plover. This species, it was said, was introduced by the great king Brian Boru, because he believed that such wary birds would give the alarm when an enemy army approached the country!

_____

A wandering voice

The cuckoo reintroduces itself into the country in late spring of each year, and is welcomed as a harbinger of good weather. However, some ambiguity was attached to its call: if a person first heard it in his right ear, he would have good fortune during the summer; but if in his left ear, it meant the opposite. The corncrake is also welcomed, though in recent times it has become a rarity in Ireland. A curious item of lore regarding this bird is that it lies on its back when calling, with its feet upwards, thinking that in this way it keeps the sky from falling!

_____

Thou shalt not kill

It was considered very unlucky to kill a swallow, and the belief was that the cows' milk would become bloody as a result. Neither should a swan be killed, for it was thought that some swans were transformed people. This idea probably arose from the peculiar human-like cry of swans, but also had links to the story in medieval Irish literature of the children of the mythical King Lir, who were transformed into swans by their jealous stepmother. Although this story did not feature much in traditional folklore, it has become well known in recent generations from story-books.

Health, wealth and wisdom

By far the most celebrated fish is the salmon. Its high leap has long been taken as a symbol of agility, and a favourite wish in Irish is for 'the health of the salmon, a heart wholesome and enduring, and to die in Ireland'. A famous story in Irish literature and folklore tells of how Fionn Mac Cumhaill got his great wisdom by eating a fine salmon from the river Boyne. Fionn himself was a remarkable athlete as well as a seer, agility in mind and body being his desired object. Parents, indeed, still advise their children to eat fish before school examinations so as to clear the mind.

Minute functionaries

Because their singing behind the fireplace suggested warmth and contentment, crickets were thought to bring good fortune to a house. However, some believed that if they were suddenly heard in the dwelling, after a long silence, this was a portent of death for a member of the family. This idea may have resulted from a confusion with the death-watch beetle, the clicking of which in libraries is generally considered an omen of death.

Curiously, fleas were by many people thought to be lucky in a house, keeping illness at bay since, like the leech, they extracted impurities from the blood.

Little friends

The robin was held in high regard, as this bird was said to have got its red breast through its efforts to stanch the blood on the brow of Jesus on the Cross. The hedgehog was also thought to have endeavoured to help the Saviour, bringing Him an apple on its spikes after His forty days of fasting. The fact that the spider helps to control the spread of flies made it a valued insect, and this was underlined in folklore by a story that it had hidden Christ from His enemies by covering Him with its web. As a result, people believed that a spider brought luck to a house, and they would never harm it.

Little foes

For some reason, the wren was considered a cursed bird, a rather unfair belief which was also common in some other areas of western Europe. It was said that it betrayed the first Christian martyr, St Stephen, by beating its wings on the drums of sleeping soldiers to alert them when Stephen passed by as a fugitive. It was symbolically hunted on the feast-day of the saint, a tradition which many scholars think evolved from an ancient ritual of expelling the spirit of winter.

Disapproval of the wren may have been compounded by its tiny size and low flying, which led to its being imagined as a kind of disguised insect. Also, being a very fertile little fellow, it was regarded as promiscuous, which would not have endeared it to the more puritanical type of Christian preacher. The upright tail of the wren accords with the same sexual imagery, as does that of the black chafer, which raises its tail when threatened. The chafer (known in Irish as *daradaol* or *deargadaol*) was also given an anti-Christian significance. It was said to have informed on Christ — thereby leading to His capture — and to be the only insect to enter the tomb of the dead Saviour.

Realms of mystery

The belief in an other-world community, which shares the environment with us but is not necessarily visible to us, is found in many old cultures. Early Irish literature tells of how people, after death, live on in such a world parallel to our own, and can intermingle with human life at special times, or when they wish to do so. These ancestors were said, naturally, to have their residences in the burial mounds or tumuli.

The ancient Irish word for a tumulus was *sídh*, and in time this word was taken to refer also to the actual inhabitants of the tumuli. So, in Irish folklore, the other-world community is referred to as the people of the *sídh* (in modern spelling, *sí*). Due to a combination of respect and fear, however, this word for them is usually avoided, and circumlocutions are used — such as *na daoine maithe* (the good people) and *na daoine uaisle* (the nobles). In ordinary speech, even those designations may not be used, and the members of the other-world referred to simply as 'they' and 'them'. The common term for them in English is 'the fairies', but this term is also avoided in Irish folk speech.

The living landscape

The general tendency is for superstition to situate these spiritual beings in features of the landscape which are cultural rather than natural. In the same way as the early Irish located the Celtic deities in old burial sites — for instance, Newgrange in Co. Meath — so the folk sensed that ancient constructions were the proper place for the fairies. Throughout Ireland, there are many earthenwork forts, or 'raths' — actually the remains of early dwelling-sites. It was widely believed that these raths were inhabited by the fairies.

Medieval Irish literature explains this belief by saying that a spiritual people, known as *Tuatha Dé Danann*, were defeated in battle by our Irish ancestors, and accepted the terms of a treaty

whereby they would live in underground dwellings.
This, however, was learned invention. The earlier
tradition must have been that both deities and the
dead had their residences in sacred places.
Something of this survives in the frequent folk
statements that sites such as hilltop cairns are
inhabited by the fairies.

The world beside us

Music can sometimes be heard at night from places
reputed to be fairy-dwellings, as the other-world
community engages in feasting and dancing inside,
and a late traveller might even see a great hurling-
match being played by them in the field beside a
rath. As a further reflection of human culture, the
fairies were believed to farm their mystical
livestock, and some stories tell of a fairy man
coming to buy and sell at an ordinary market.
However, any money which he handed over by way
of transaction was likely to turn into withered
leaves as soon as he left!

There were tales of individuals who, ignoring
fairy sensibilities, levelled or dug up a rath, and met
with some misfortune as a result. In a similar vein, a
solitary tree standing in the middle of a field —
particularly a whitethorn — was thought to be a
crann sí (fairy tree) and to be especially dear to the
fairies. If such a tree were cut down, the offender was
liable soon to meet with an accident, or even death.

Old Irish literature tells of how the *Tuatha Dé* sometimes fought battles among themselves, and it is not surprising to find this idea also associated with the fairies in superstitions. Noises heard at night could be interpreted in this way, as well as prehistoric arrowheads found near raths. Milk or any other light-coloured substance seen on the ground in the morning might be interpreted as blood spilt during these battles, for fairy blood was believed to be white.

By invitation only

Just as the old literature describes how the *Tuatha Dé* took human heroes into their world in order to help them in their battles, so folklore describes the fairies taking good hurlers away overnight to join their teams. They also carried off accomplished musicians to provide entertainment at their feasts. The most sumptuous food was offered to the human visitor there, but if he partook of it, he would never be able to return to his worldly existence.

Fine gifts from the beyond

Again like the *Tuatha Dé* of old, the fairies were believed sometimes to bestow artistic gifts upon humans, especially skill at music or in poetry. Many stories told of how a great musician or poet first got his talent when he fell asleep one night on a fairy rath. Several such artists were blind or of poor sight in traditional Ireland, and this social reality was explained by the assertion that they had lost their sight after a fairy vision. Particularly in the case of a poet, it was claimed that a beautiful fairy lady was the donor of the gift, and the light emanating from her was so strong that he was blinded.

Crossing the bridge

Perhaps as a remnant of the veneration for the dead in ancient times, and of the tradition that they lived on in a neighbourly other-world, there was a vestige of belief that those who died joined the fairy world. It was sometimes said that, upon the death of a person, a door would be heard to close in a hillside. A very popular folk legend tells of how a young woman died, and after her burial appeared in a dream to her husband and told him that she would be passing with a fairy cavalcade at a certain place and at a certain time. She instructed him to bring a black-hafted knife, and to plunge it into the horse on which she was riding. This would effect her escape and return to life. When the husband met the cavalry, however, he hesitated, and so she was lost to him forever.

To a place unknown

Many people believed in fairy abduction, and
especially regarding children and mothers after
childbirth, this was a ready-to-hand explanation of
unexpected and mysterious ailments. A healthy
child or young woman who suddenly began to
pine was thought to be in the process of being
taken away by the fairies.

A common European legend was imported into
Ireland some centuries ago to dramatise this belief.
According to the legend, a family friend noticed
that the appearance of a baby had changed
significantly, and discovered that the real baby had
in fact been taken by the fairies and a miserable
changeling left in its place. When he heated the
tongs in the fire and threatened the changeling
with it, the latter raced from the cradle, out the
door, and into a nearby fairy rath. In a short time,
the real baby was mysteriously returned to the
family, as safe and well as ever.

Let them stay

Irish lore of the *sí* has, in fact, been much
influenced by medieval notions in other European
countries concerning the fairy world. One such
notion was that the fairies are some of the angels
who rebelled against God and were expelled from
Heaven as a result. After His initial wrath, the

Almighty relented somewhat and said that these angels need not fall any lower than the point at which they then were. So, we are told, the fairies are the angels who had reached the level of the earth. Others had fallen into the sea — which ties in well with the many Irish stories which have humans being transported to other-world dwellings across or even underneath the sea.

Hill and house

According to a legend told of many hills in Ireland, but especially of Slievenamon in Co. Tipperary, three fairy women tried to abduct a woman from her house, but she tricked them by persuading them to help her with the spinning-wheel. She then rushed to the door and, feigning alarm, said that the top of the hill was on fire. Fearing that their dwelling there was ablaze, the fairy women raced out of the house, and the woman slammed the door shut. She prevented them from returning by keeping the dirty washing-water in the house from that time onwards. The fairies, being very fastidious, would not go near a place where dirty water was kept.

The little celebrity

The motif of outwitting by means of a trick occurs in another very common Irish legend, though in this the tables are turned. It concerns the leprechaun, a diminutive but well-dressed little fellow sometimes claimed to be shoemaker to the fairies. He is said to have a hidden crock of gold, the whereabouts of which he will disclose if he is caught and kept within sight. According to the legend, a man caught him once and, holding him firmly in his grasp, demanded to know where the treasure was. The quick-witted leprechaun, however, shouted out that a fearsome animal was approaching the man from behind, and the man turned away to look. There was, of course, no such animal, but when the man looked back again, the leprechaun was gone!

This elusive fellow — who is generally alone when encountered — seems to derive from ideas in early European literature concerning treasure-guarding dwarves. His original name in Irish was *luchorpán*, meaning 'small-bodied fellow', and he is known by local corruptions of this in different parts of Ireland — such as *luchramán*, *clúracán*, *loimreachán*, *lurgadán* and *luchragán*, as well as *leipreachán*.

Lonely cry at night

The most famous of all other-world beings in Ireland is the banshee (from the Irish *bean sí*: other-world woman). She is a distinctively Gaelic personage, and probably evolved from old ideas of

the land-goddess as patroness of kings and
chieftains. In folk belief, her wailing cry is heard
near to the dwelling-house when a member of the
family is about to die.

This belief is still very strong in Ireland, and
dwellers in towns and cities claim to hear the
banshee before a death, just as people in rural areas
do. She even seems to keep abreast of the fortunes
of the Irish all over the world, for many claim to
have heard her lamentation, without any apparent
cause, only to learn soon afterwards that a relative
had died abroad.

The great survivor

The banshee is hardly ever seen, and those people
who claim to have caught a fleeting glimpse of her
are not in agreement as to her appearance. Some
say that she is a haggard-looking little woman,
while others claim that she is a fine, fair-haired
lady with a long cloak. This contrast in
appearances, in fact, parallels descriptions of the
goddess of sovereignty in old Irish literature —
where the lady Ireland is young and beautiful when
the country prospers but is old and miserable in
times of misfortune.

That the banshee is a survival of ancient
tradition is further indicated by the name she is
given in the folklore of south Leinster: *badhbh*
(pronounced 'bow') or *badhbh chaointe* ('bo-

heentha'). Badhbh was the name of a goddess in early Ireland who appeared in the form of a crow and screamed over battlefields.

FOUR

RULES AND PRACTICE OF LIFE

*S*uperstitions tend to emphasise certain points in *time and place, and also curious images and actions. This is a development of the natural propensity to learn, whereby striking phenomena are selected as representative of others less striking. However, the appeal of drama to human emotions means that such things are invested with a higher intensity of meaning, and accorded a particular status in superstitious thought.*

Living it to the full

With regard to time, intensity is attributed to special points in two basic spheres: the personal and the seasonal — that is, special points in the life of the individual person and special points in the passing of the year. In traditional understanding, the three basic points in the life of a person are birth, marriage and death, and it is not surprising that many superstitions cluster around these three.

New life

The birth of a child was a matter of great social importance and, as both imagination and tradition will always have it, this was expressed in mystical terms. It was said in Ireland that sterility could be overcome by a couple's sleeping on top of a dolmen, the remains of an ancient burial chamber, which consisted of a fairly flat stone placed across upright ones. These dolmens are found in many parts of the country, and the common term for one was *Leaba Dhiarmada agus Ghráinne* — the bed of Diarmaid Ó Duibhne and Gráinne. It was said that the eloping lovers, in their flight from Fionn Mac Cumhaill and his men, slept in the relative safety of these raised 'beds'.

There were thought to be many external dangers to conception. For instance, if an enemy tied a knot in a handkerchief when two people were married, no child would be born to the couple until the malicious knot were opened. It was widely believed that a pregnant woman should avoid meeting a hare, for if one crossed her path, her child would be born with its most noticeable attribute, a 'hare-lip'. This could be prevented, however, if the woman tore the hem of her skirt when she saw the hare, thus transferring the blemish from the child's mouth to the clothing.

The time of travail

A pregnant woman should not attend a wake, as it was feared that proximity to a corpse might attract death to the unborn child. This is an example of the principle, strong in folk belief, that things contiguous to each other can have an effect on each other. A pregnant woman should also avoid entering a graveyard, for if she stepped over a grave, the child would be born with a twisted foot.

Versions of the far-flung rite known as 'couvade', which consisted of an attempt by the father to take the pains of childbirth away from his wife, were known in Ireland. Thus a woman about to bear a child might wear a waistcoat or some other item of clothing belonging to her husband, in the belief that this would transfer the pains to him. Alternatively, the man might do some special type of heavy work until the birth — like digging a rough garden or drawing bucket after bucket of water from the well — in order to attract to himself the physical exhaustion. These are examples of an idea which is often at work in folk thought — that there is limited energy in the world and that this energy can only be shared, not increased or diminished.

Wish of parents

When it came to the birth itself, the importance of time was particularly stressed. A child born at night was said to have the power of seeing ghosts and fairies, and if fortunate enough to be born at the stroke of midnight, would be very intelligent, perhaps even a poet of excellence. In Ireland, as abroad, special notice was taken of a child born with a 'caul', called *caipín an tsonais* (cap of happiness), and he was thought destined to have great good fortune in life. Some people went so far as to preserve the caul for good luck or even for use in cures.

For some reason, it was considered unlucky for a child to be born on Whit Sunday, for he would grow up either to kill or to be killed. To avoid this fate, an unfortunate worm would be crushed in such a baby's hand after birth, as the destined killing was then deemed to have been done.

Pairing off

Marriage was also a crucial time in human life, and there was a strong feeling in traditional Ireland that a person did not really come of age and become a full adult member of the community until he married. Many superstitions centred on the wedding ceremony. For instance, certain days of the week — such as Monday or Friday — were believed unlucky for it. Similarly, the colour green was unlucky, and should not be worn by the bride. It was also considered unlucky if it rained, if a glass or cup were broken on the morning before the wedding, if a dog licked either groom or bride, if the wedding-ring fell to the floor during the ceremony, or if somebody kissed the bride before the groom did so.

There were certain customs which were thought to bring good luck to the newly married couple — throwing something after them as they left the church, for instance, or throwing coins into the air over their heads. It was, indeed, usual for youngsters attending the wedding to gather outside the church door and tussle for the money as it fell. When the newly-weds reached their house, it was believed to bring them good luck if a man, rather than a woman, were the first to greet them, and of course the groom was supposed to carry the bride over the threshold, as a symbol of the gentility which a man should show towards his wife.

The race for happiness

In some parts of the country, all the able-bodied men would race from the church gate, or from some other convenient point, to the house of the couple. This race might take place on horseback, in which case the men's wives would be seated behind them. This was called 'the race for the bottle', the prize usually being a bottle of whiskey on a wall near the house. Once the bride entered her new home, the mother-in-law would break a cake of bread over her head, as a token that she would henceforth be the mistress of baking and other domestic business in her new dwelling.

The wheel of sorrow

The last point of great importance is, of course, death, the supreme negative. As an old saying in Irish has it, 'There is no herb or cure for death.' Death was sometimes personified as a sombre spectrum seen lingering about the dwelling of the destined person. There were other images, such as a cloud formation looking like a funeral cortège in the sky, which presaged a death in the locality. The unavoidable reality of death was dramatised by a very old belief in Ireland, that of *fód an bháis* (the sod of death). It was fancifully claimed that a particular sod was predestined for each person, and that in this way we will all die on our own 'sods'. This, of course, was especially suitable as an explanation for a tragic or unexpected death.

In the case of fatal illness, relatives of the sick person would generally be tense, and become conscious of somewhat unusual things in the surroundings which normally might go unnoticed. These were then interpreted as portents of death: for instance, a bird perching on the window-sill, a dog howling at night, a scald-crow flying over the house, a picture which chanced to fall from the wall, or even bees leaving their hive. And, of course, any strange high-pitched sound heard outside might be taken for the cry of the banshee.

The final resolution

Care was taken to keep the household fire burning, as a weakening of it was believed to cause a diminution in the health of the patient. If a dying person felt discomfort or pain, it was often ascribed to the presence of the feather of a wild bird in the mattress, and the patient would be moved to another bed.

As the ailing person expired, doors and windows would be opened and, in olden times, a hole would be made in the thatch of the house, so as to ease the passing of the soul. Nobody present would stand or kneel between the dying person and these exits. The soul was thought to leave the body through the crown of the head, but it might linger a little in the house, and so relatives and friends refrained for a while from keening or lamenting.

No going back

When a person died, the household clock would be stopped, mirrors turned to the wall, and any pet animals in the house put out. The origin of these customs must be some form of belief in reincarnation — that is, a fear that the soul or 'spirit' of the dead person might pass into some potential body, such as an object which moved or showed variation. After some time, the windows were closed and the curtains drawn — presumably to prevent the departed soul from returning to the house.

There was definitely a certain amount of fear of the dead in traditional folk belief. For example, roundabout ways were taken by the funeral procession to the cemetery, and in some places the coffin was carried around the graveyard a few times before burial. The origin of this custom must have been to put astray the ghost of the dead person lest it return to reassert its role in the affairs of the living. This, as with most explanations for folk customs and beliefs, has been forgotten. Indeed, it is not by rationale that folklore survives, but by repetition. Veneration grows for something which is so often performed that it becomes traditional; as the old saying in Irish goes, *Ná déan nós agus ná bris nós* (Don't make a custom and don't break a custom).

Remaining with us

The most important way of all for the community to express its concern for the dead was the custom of waking: that is, keeping the body of the deceased in his own dwelling until burial. The wakes were great social occasions. Neighbours and friends congregated in the house in the evening, and stories were told, songs were sung, music and dancing took place, and many games were played to while away the night.

The dead person was not only lamented loudly in these old wakes, but often addressed as if alive. The tobacco-pipe was extended to the corpse as it was to all the adults present, and when card-games were played it might even be given its own hand. The most plausible explanation for these strange practices is that an attempt was being made to reassure the dead person that he was not being rejected by the community, and therefore had no need to feel peeved.

Journey into the unknown

These notions are, of course, somewhat at variance with Christian tradition, and for that reason were often censured by the clergy. But old ideas, particularly when they are concerned with such a crucial human issue as death, themselves die hard. Other survivals of ancient traditions include the belief that one should not wear the clothes of a deceased relative for some time after his death, and the custom of leaving food on the grave for a few days after a burial. The soul, it was said, was on its way to the afterlife, travelling a long and cold road, and thus needed its clothes and sustenance.

The season of gloom

The November Festival had much ancient ritual associated with the dead. Marking the beginning of

the cold, wet and dark season of winter, it was a time when the living stayed indoors as much as possible. In the old literature, the eerie nature of *Oíche Shamhna* (Hallowe'en) was conveyed by accounts of cairns and other-world dwellings being open at that time, and of the adventures of ordinary folk who entered them.

The belief persists that ghosts of the dead are more likely to be encountered at Hallowe'en. Until recently, many people retired to bed early on that night, leaving food and drink on the table for their dead relatives, who it was thought might return to spend the night in the kitchen of their old houses. It was also believed that on Hallowe'en night the spirits of the dead came from the graveyard to the local church, and spent some time praying there. Much of this lore has now become attached to the Church feast of All Souls, two days later.

The two sides

The Irish year was basically divided into two parts, as the old saying goes, *ó Shamhain go Bealtaine is ó Bhealtaine go Samhain* (from November to May and from May to November). May, as the beginning of summer, symbolised the coming of good weather and of agricultural gain. Since folk thought tends to look upon beginnings as presaging what follows, people were anxious that all indications would be good at this time. Nobody would give any belongings away on May Eve, and anybody who asked for such was believed to be trying to steal a neighbour's good fortune. One who asked for a loan of salt, or who took lighting from the household fire, was immediately suspect.

Superstition was especially strong regarding matters which involved no certainty, such as milk, hay and crops. The dew on fields in the morning has long been a symbol of agricultural prosperity, and it was thought that greedy or malicious people might try to gather some from a neighbour's field before dawn on May Eve. Similarly, they might try to skim the top layer of water off a neighbour's well, and some farmers would stay up all night guarding their properties from such a foray.

A common legend told of a family which found that, despite all its efforts, its milk would not convert to butter on May Eve. To remedy this, the red-hot coulter of a plough was placed in the churn, and immediately a neighbour came screaming to the house, begging to be released from a terrible stomach-pain. This was the neighbour who had placed the hostile charm on the churn.

The protective saints

The beginnings of the other two seasons, spring and autumn, had customs of their own attached to them. The first day of February was anciently called *oímelg* (which meant lactation), and introduced the season of birth of young animals. It has long been known in Ireland as the Feast of St Brigid, who is the special patroness of cattle. Crosses were woven from rushes in her honour at this time, and placed in the cattle-byre as a protection for the animals. Also, a piece of cloth would be left outside the house on the eve of the feast, as it was believed that the saint passed by during the night and would bless it. This, the *brat Bhríde* (Brigid's cloak), was afterwards kept as a talisman.

The autumn festival celebrated the start of harvesting, and was called *Lughnasa*, after the ancient Celtic god Lugh. In folk tradition, it too has become Christianised, and is said to commemorate the conversion by St Patrick of a great apocryphal pagan called Crom Dubh. At this time, people were in celebratory mood, climbing hilltops, or assembling at rivers and lakes and taking part in outdoor sports. Bilberries or whortleberries (*fraocháin*) were picked and eaten, these being symbolic of the first fruits of the harvest.

The surviving spirit

The good farmer tried to have his harvest saved before September. As the work neared its end, special attention was paid to the cutting of the last sheaf. In most of the north and of the midlands, this was called the *cailleach* (hag), and the belief was that a hare retreated before the mowers and took up its last hiding-place within it. It is easy to distinguish here an original idea concerning a spirit of the harvest.

In some places, indeed, this last sheaf was thought to have magical properties, and would be brought home and hung in the dwelling-house or barn for good luck. However, it was said that some malicious individuals could make a very special use of their own of this sheaf. They would steal it and bury it in the ground, and as it decayed, so too would the health of the rightful owner. In such a case, the only cure was for the owner to find it again and burn it.

Bright and powerful

With regard to agricultural luck and prosperity, mention should also be made of the bonfires of midsummer, or St John's Night. In Ireland, as elsewhere in Europe, people assembled around these fires and danced, sang and made merry. It was customary in some parts of the country to drive the cattle between two bonfires, in the expectation that this would protect them from disease, and for young men and women to jump over the corners of the fires in order to guarantee marriage and fertility. When the bonfires had died down, their embers were scattered on the fields and haggards in the belief that this would bring about growth — a further illustration of the supernatural power often attributed to fire.

The appeal of religion

The two major Church festivals, Easter and
Christmas, have much lore attached to them. No
nails were driven into timber on Good Friday, out
of respect for Christ's death, and women would let
their hair hang loose as a sign of sorrow. Since
Christ's death was redemptive, it was considered a
great blessing for an ailing person to depart this life
on Good Friday. Also as an echo of the Gospels, it
was thought that if a gale arose on this day, it
would abate on Easter Sunday.

Christmas, as the day commemorating the birth
of the Saviour, was of paramount importance in
traditional Irish life. It was believed that the gates of
Heaven were open at this time, and that anybody
who died during the twelve days of Christmas had
an easy passage there. On Christmas Eve itself, a
special candle was lit in the window, as a symbolic
guide to the Holy Family wandering the lonely
roads outside as they had on the first Christmas. It
was said that, in memory of the holy birth, all of
creation rejoiced at midnight on Christmas Eve,
and that the donkeys and cows briefly got the gift
of speech to praise the divine child.

Marvels of the mind

Another imaginative tradition of high order was
connected with the Epiphany, known in Ireland as

Little Christmas or Women's Christmas. As the twelve days came to their conclusion, at midnight of this festival, three colourful transformations fleetingly took place — the water in the well became wine, the rushes became silk and the sandstone became gold. A human should not go out of his way to observe these marvels, however, and humorous stories were told of topers who were so audacious as to drink the transformed water and were turned into stone as a result!

Times good and bad

The unluckiest date, according to Irish superstition, was 28 December, when the slaughter of the Holy Innocents was commemorated. This was known as 'the forbidden day of the year', and no new enterprise was undertaken upon it. Conversely, New Year's Day was a good date for starting a task, as it was felt to cast its influence on all of the year that followed it.

A new beginning

In former times, it was customary for the family to have a big meal on New Year's Eve, and to throw a cake against the kitchen door so as to banish hunger. On New Year's Day itself, special notice was taken of the weather, as this was thought to betoken the general trend during the ensuing year.

Some people even thought that the economic prospects could be ascertained by placing a stick in the river: if the water-level fell, it was welcomed as an indication of a decrease in prices; if it rose, inflation was in store!

Many things seen or experienced in the New Year were taken to presage the future. For instance, if the first horse seen by a person had its head towards him, that was a sign of good luck, but its rear meant bad luck. To find a horseshoe on the road augured well for the year, but it had to be turned towards the person in order to channel the good fortune in his direction. Similarly, it was considered auspicious to discover a pin on the road on one's first trip outdoors on New Year's Day, provided also that it is pointing towards the observer.

The day of rest

Note was taken of the days of the week, and particular traits associated with them. Sunday was in many ways the most important. Since Church rules forbade unnecessary servile work on this day, it was believed that work carried out was unlucky and always proved futile. Furthermore, people should not work too near to the junctures — *buille déanach an tSathairn agus buille luath an Luain* (the late stroke on Saturday and the early stroke on Monday) must be avoided. If absolutely necessary, a woman might put a stitch in a garment on

Sunday, but she would be careful to replace it with a new stitch on the following day.

Children born on Sunday were expected to be of a saintly disposition. Herbs picked then were said to be more effective in curing ailments, and it was thought that the fairies could not overhear human conversation on the Lord's Day. On a more mundane level, since it is the first day of the week, many farmers thought it a good day on which to change the cattle from one pasture to another.

One day at a time

For some reason, Monday was thought unsuitable for any new undertaking. If a field had to be ploughed on that day, the first sod would be turned on the preceding Saturday, and if a grave had to be dug, one sod would be cut on the Sunday. It was believed inadvisable to part with money on that day — in fact, people even avoided sweeping the dust out of the house on a Monday, for fear they would be giving their good luck away!

Tuesday, on the other hand, was a good day to begin a job, and was strongly recommended for churning butter or for any type of spinning. Many people considered it the luckiest day of the week, and it was an especially popular one for weddings — probably because of the importance of Shrove Tuesday as the last day before Lent on which a marriage would be solemnised.

Things repeated

Wednesday was regarded as the best day for buying and selling, and also for moving house or for travel. Seafarers, indeed, placed great trust in this day, as it was thought usually to presage a change for the better in the weather; the old saying was, *Ní théann stoirm thar Dhomhnach ná rabharta thar Chéadaoin* (A storm does not last longer than Sunday nor a swell longer than Wednesday). There was one notable exception to this good fortune, namely Spy Wednesday, which was considered a most unlucky day because of its commemoration of the betrayal of Christ.

A time for healing

Thursday was also a good day for markets and for any other kind of commercial transaction, but its particular importance lay in the realm of curing illnesses. People preferred this day for visits to the local doctor or healer, and in a similar vein, many made a habit of washing and shaving on Thursday. There may be echoes in all of this of Christ's celebration of the Last Supper and institution of the Eucharist.

Because of the Crucifixion, Friday was a day on which it was thought that people should take special care at their prayers. It was also considered a very good day for starting new work — but never for marrying, as this would be too joyful and festive an event. Since there was an association between Friday and storms, people were loth to go to sea on that day.

The weekend break

Coming at the end of a hard week's work, Saturday found people in good spirits, and it was said that the sun would never fail to shine then, at least for a brief period. In many areas, indeed, it was regarded as a day especially devoted to the Blessed Virgin. The injunction has it thus, *Fág an Satharn ag Muire Mháthair!* (Leave the Saturday to Mother Mary!) Accordingly, it was a sort of second day of rest and, although housework and other necessary chores were recommended, large undertakings like the beginning of house-building or the launch of a new boat were considered unlucky.

Counting with care

The week is a cultural rather than a natural unit of time, and its importance in the folk mind is in large part due to its division into seven days. Particular importance is attributed to the number seven in many cultures. In Ireland, several preternatural occurrences — such as visions of fairy dwellings — were said to take place every seven years.

Children were said first to show their individual abilities at the age of seven, and on the darker side, a curse on a family was believed to run for seven generations. The seventh son of a seventh son was thought to have extraordinary healing powers, probably due to the rareness of such a person in the community. Likewise, a posthumous child — also comparatively rare — was said to have the gift of healing.

How many times?

Of the other numbers, three was the most important in Ireland. This is a very old belief, for the early literature refers to several Celtic deities who were triplicate. Major events in folk stories often occur three times, and triads figure prominently in Irish proverbs. This number has connotations of roundness and totality, and many ritual acts — such as walking around a bonfire on St John's Night or doing rounds at a holy well — were performed thrice. If one dreamed of the same thing on three nights running, this was taken as proof that the dream was true.

Mystery and silence

Hidden treasures of the personality, like the know-how of healing, were usually kept secret, a tradition reinforced by the belief that such a gift, if divulged, would desert its possessor. Similarly, it was held that secrets concerning the private affairs of others should be kept, misfortune befalling the person who broke this rule. No small effort might be involved in thus keeping good faith, for it was thought that a secret could cause its possessor great stress and even failure of health. To avoid this, he might confide it to an innocent witness, such as an animal, tree, stone, or hole in the wall.

Choosing words carefully

The ideal of mutual dependence has always been a mark of Irish life, and this is reflected in beliefs concerning the use of speech. Some words could cause harm, even if uttered without bad intent. For instance, one should not carelessly say, 'God bless the work' to those digging a grave, nor should one welcome a neighbour to a wake. And nobody should ever utter an oath such as 'May I die if this is not true!'

When wishing for good fortune, a person should be as inclusive as possible, for the *guí ghann* (stingy prayer) could cause ill luck to befall those for whom it was made. The idea was that such a wish contained an element of jealousy. A person who scoffed at the handicap of another, or who compared the traits of a fellow to those of an animal, was thought to be inviting harm onto himself. Similarly, mimicry was frowned upon, and thought potentially dangerous to those who engaged in it, for as the saying goes, 'Mocking is catching.'

A curious belief concerning *uair na hachainí* (the time of wishing) claimed that there was a certain time in each day at which, if one expressed a wish, it would be granted. A story was told about an old woman who, seeking to avail of this, prayed continuously one day that her son would become King of Ireland. During her prayers, a large lump of soot fell from the chimney into the fireplace, and she exclaimed, 'Blast you, chimney!' It immediately took fire, almost destroying the house, and she barely escaped with her life.

Resources of the environment

Many objects were believed to bring good luck and to banish misfortune. Iron was, in Ireland as abroad, believed to be especially powerful in this regard, and because he worked with iron, the blacksmith was considered a wise counsellor with powers of healing. He could banish ailments, and even spirits, by pointing a piece of red-hot iron in their direction, or by turning the anvil towards them. Water used for cooling iron in the forge was thought to have properties of healing, especially in the case of warts. Another type of water much in demand was that blessed in the church at Easter — people would sprinkle this on the boundaries of their properties to protect their good fortune.

Some emphasis was placed on directions. For instance, to sleep facing eastwards invited death, as graves were usually in that position. To sleep facing northwards ensured good health, presumably because it might acclimatise one to the harsh weather which the north wind represented. No doubt because of its association with the sun, it was thought lucky to change residence southwards, except on Mondays or Fridays. The west, representing the sunset, was usually associated with decline, and it was considered proper that the room furthest west in the house should be occupied by the oldest member of the family.

Junctures in space, as those in time, were given special importance in folk thought. To enter a new part of the landscape, indeed, could easily be assimilated to the experience of entering a new stage of one's life. Crossroads and bridges were accordingly thought to be places where either good or bad fortune might be encountered. Several stories told of people who met with ghosts at such locations, but the landscape also offered remedies to such predicaments, for it was commonly held that spirits could not cross running water or a boundary between two townlands.

Power unbroken

The belief that lines enclosed power was especially strong in the case of a circle, the symbol of totality. A healer treating a skin ailment would often draw a circle around it in red ink, claiming that the

malfunction would be confined within that area.
Similarly, a gold ring was applied to the eye to cure
a sty or to the tooth to ease toothache. It was
sometimes said that if one looked through such a
ring the fairies could be seen, for a gold ring, being
small and colourful, was felt to have a kind of
microscopic effect and so provide a window onto
the flitting spiritual world. Fanciful as they are,
superstitions entail a large degree not only of
calculation but of silhouetting, which accounts for
the strong visual sense lying behind many of them.

The artist within

People would often argue at length over whether
meeting with a black cat indicated good or bad
luck. However, while the interpretation was not
definitive, the image was a constant, the striking
mental picture of an animal so black as to stand
out vividly from its surroundings.

The part played by colour in superstition seems
to be at all times connected with the 'visual'
sharpening of the imagination.

This is further illustrated by superstitions
concerning the colour red. This colour was, on the
one hand, taken to be a bad omen in the case of a
fox or a red-haired woman encountered before
going on the sea, but had a positive function when
a red ribbon was attached to a child or a farm

animal in order to repel illness or to prevent damage by the evil eye. White too had long associations with the other-world, and had equally ambiguous power. A white cow, for instance, was said to bring bad luck to a herd, but dressing children in white clothes was thought to protect them from being taken into the fairy world.

In paying tribute to this 'aesthetic' tendency in superstition, we conclude by citing the three unluckiest things to gaze upon early in the morning: 'a white horse, a house on a height and a fine woman'. Noting the fact that these rhyme (*capall bán, tigh ar ard agus bean bhreá*), we may doubt the negative interpretation, and instead appreciate the attractive imagery of all three against the background of a dull and dreary daybreak.

INDEX